LOVE AMONG THE HAYSTACKS

When the grass is tall and sweet and full of summer sunshine, it is time to cut it down and make hay – hay that will hold that summer sweetness all through the cold, hungry winter months. But the work must be done quickly, to keep the new hay safe from wind and rain. Every farmer knows this.

Geoffrey and Maurice know it too. They are farmer's sons, and work hard, building the haystack. But what do these young men think about, while they work under the hot summer sun? They think about a girl, a German girl called Paula, a girl in a yellow dress, a girl with bright eyes and a funny, quick way of talking. They can see her now, up the hill, in the garden of a house next to the hayfield. Maurice has kissed her, but Geoffrey has not, and Geoffrey burns with hate for his brother. He finds words difficult. No woman will ever love him, he thinks, because he cannot find the words to win her love.

But love does not always need words, and who knows what the day or the night will bring? Paula is not the only young woman to visit the hayfield that day . . .

OXFORD BOOKWORMS LIBRARY

Classics

Love among the Haystacks

Stage 2 (700 headwords)

Series Editor: Jennifer Bassett
Founder Editor: Tricia Hedge
Activities Editors: Jennifer Bassett and Christine Lindop

D. H. LAWRENCE

Love among the Haystacks

Retold by
Jennifer Bassett

Illustrated by
Bob Harvey

OXFORD UNIVERSITY PRESS

OXFORD

UNIVERSITY PRESS

Great Clarendon Street, Oxford, OX2 6DP, United Kingdom

Oxford University Press is a department of the University of Oxford.
It furthers the University's objective of excellence in research, scholarship,
and education by publishing worldwide. Oxford is a registered trade
mark of Oxford University Press in the UK and in certain other countries

ISBN: 978 0 19 479080 2   Book
ISBN: 978 0 19 463764 0   Book and audio pack

Printed in China

Word count (main text): 7,030 words

For more information on the Oxford Bookworms Library,
visit www.oup.com/elt/gradedreaders

ACKNOWLEDGEMENTS

Text adaptation by Jennifer Bassett

Illustrated by Bob Harvey

Cover image by Tatsiana Volskaya courtesy of Moment Open/Getty Images

CONTENTS

1

Two brothers

The two large fields lay on a hillside that looked south. Most of the hay was already cut, and in the bright sunlight the fields were now golden green.

Across the hill, half-way up, was a high hedge, and they were building the haystack just above this hedge. It was a tall haystack, a great untidy thing standing high above the hedge, but the hay itself was light and silvery in colour, and looked as soft as a cloud. Not far away was another, finished haystack.

The empty wagon was going downhill, and in the far corner of the bottom field, where the hay was still uncut, the full wagon was just beginning its slow journey up the hill to the haystack. The hay-makers worked on, cutting the tall hay, while the wagon climbed the hill.

The two brothers on top of the haystack were having a moment's rest, waiting for the full wagon to arrive. They stood up to their knees in the soft hay, while above them the golden sun burned down, and all around them was the hot sweet smell of the silvery hay. The only two things in the world were hay and sun.

1

Maurice, the younger brother, was a good-looking young man of twenty-one. He was strong, full of life, with a quick bright eye and a ready smile.

'You thought,' he said to his brother, 'you were very clever last night, didn't you?' He pushed his fork into the hay, and stared at his brother, with a smile on his face.

'No. No, I didn't,' replied Geoffrey. He turned away, frowning. He was a tall, heavy young man, a year older than Maurice. He was full of strong feelings, but they burned silently inside him. He could never find words to say; he could never look anybody in the eye. He always thought the world was looking at him, and laughing.

'Oh, you did, I know you did.' Maurice laughed. 'It was your turn to sleep in the hayfield last night, but you went and hid yourself, so I had to go in your place.'

'I didn't hide myself,' said Geoffrey angrily. 'Father sent me to get some wood—'

'Oh yes, oh yes,' laughed Maurice. 'But you don't know, do you? You don't know what happened last night, up here in the hayfield.'

He laughed again, and threw himself down on his back in the hay. He put his arms across his face and lay there, smiling and remembering the night before.

Geoffrey leant on his fork and stared out over the fields. Far away was the city of Nottingham, and between, the country lay under the burning sun, with here and

Geoffrey leant on his fork and stared out over the fields.

there the smoke from a factory going up into the sky.
Geoffrey looked down again into the hayfield, at the
wagon slowly climbing the hill to the haystack. 'Hurry
up,' he thought. 'Hurry up.'

'You didn't think, did you?' said Maurice. 'You didn't
think that *she* would be here with me, did you?'

Geoffrey stared at him, full of hate. Suddenly, he
wanted to put his foot down hard on that smiling, good-
looking face below him.

'Can you sing in German?' asked Maurice. 'Do you
know how to kiss a German girl? Do you know how soft
her neck is?' He laughed excitedly, remembering every
moment of the night before.

Geoffrey burned with hate. He wanted to walk away,
but he couldn't. The haystack, high above the field, was a
prison holding him and his brother together.

Both brothers were shy of women. Neither of them had
a girlfriend; neither of them knew what to say to a woman,
or how to win her love. And now Maurice was first in the
game, and the older brother did not like it.

The German girl was the governess from the house
beside the top field. Geoffrey was working one day in
the field when a baby pushed through a hole in the hedge
from the garden of the house. Seconds later the German
girl came through the hedge too, looking for the baby.
Geoffrey helped her to catch the little boy, and then they stood

talking for a while. Geoffrey liked her bright eyes, and her funny, quick way of talking.

'But now it's Maurice she likes best, not me,' he thought. 'She sits with him in the hayfield by moonlight, and he kisses her.'

Unhappily, he looked up the hill to the house beside the top field. From the top of the haystack he could see right into the garden, and there, suddenly, he saw the girl, in a yellow dress. He held up his arm and waved to her. She waved back, lazily. Geoffrey could see that she was not interested in him, and was waiting for Maurice.

Then Maurice stood up, and saw the girl himself. He laughed, and waved both arms at her.

'What's going on?' called a voice from below.

The full wagon was now standing at the foot of the haystack. Maurice's face turned deep red.

'Nothing!' he called.

There was the sound of laughing below, and soon a big, red-faced man climbed to the top of the hay in the wagon. He turned, stared up the hillside, and saw the yellow dress in the garden.

'Oh, it's a girl, is it?' he laughed. He was the father of Geoffrey and Maurice. 'Yes, I *thought* it was a girl.'

They began working again, throwing the hay from the wagon up to the top of the haystack. There the brothers had to place the hay carefully, building a stack with four strong walls which would not fall over. It was hard work. The father threw up great forkfuls of hay, Geoffrey then passed them along to Maurice, who built up the haystack's walls.

But Geoffrey was full of angry feelings. Usually he threw the hay into the places where Maurice wanted it. Now, he threw it into the middle of the stack, and Maurice had to work twice as hard, carrying it out to the walls. Once, a great forkful of hay from Geoffrey hit Maurice on the back.

'Be careful!' called Maurice angrily. 'And why are you throwing it in the middle, you stupid man?'

'I'll throw it where I like,' answered Geoffrey.

They worked on, both brothers angry now. They got hotter and tireder, and still the hay came up from the wagon below.

'There, that's the end,' the father called at last from the wagon. Geoffrey threw the last forkful into the middle of the stack, then stood still, watching Maurice.

'This side wall isn't very strong,' came the father's voice from below. 'You must build it up more.'

'No, it's fine,' called Maurice crossly.

Geoffrey moved across to the side wall, and pushed his fork down into the hay. He pushed harder, and the top of the haystack began to move just a little.

'What are you doing, you fool?' cried Maurice.

'Don't you call me a fool,' said Geoffrey, and he pushed again on his fork. Maurice jumped across to him, and pulled him away from the wall. It was not easy to stand in the soft bed of hay, and Geoffrey fell over.

Maurice pulled Geoffrey away from the wall.

Maurice called down to his father below. 'This wall is fine. It's not going to fall down.'

'All right,' came the father's voice. 'We'll be off now to bring the next wagon up here.'

Geoffrey got to his feet. 'Don't call me a fool again, do you hear?' he said heavily.

'Not until next time,' said his brother.

Maurice went on working, moving round the stack and building up the walls. Geoffrey stood still, hand on his fork, looking out over the fields. He did not move even when Maurice needed to get past him.

'Move, will you?' said Maurice.

There was no reply. Maurice put out his arm and tried to push his brother out of his way.

'Who are you pushing?' said Geoffrey angrily.

'You,' replied Maurice, and at once the two brothers began to fight. Each pushed against the other as hard as he could, but Geoffrey was the heavier of the two men, and slowly he began to win.

Maurice had to move back, but his feet caught in the hay, and he fell over the side of the stack, all the way down to the ground.

2

The German girl

eoffrey's face turned white. He heard the fall. He stood still, listening. He could hear no sound from below; he could hear no sound at all, anywhere. Then he was filled with sudden terror.

'Father!' he shouted, in his great deep voice. 'Father! FATHER!'

The cry rang across the fields. Men came running from the bottom field, and a girl ran down across the upper field. Geoffrey heard her strange, wild voice.

'Ah–h!' she cried out. 'Ah–h! Are you dead?'

On the top of the stack Geoffrey did not move or speak. He was too afraid to go down, too afraid even to hide in the hay. He listened to the voices below.

First to arrive was his older brother, Henry. Then came his father, and Bill, one of the farm workers.

'What's the matter? What's happened? Oh no!'

That was his father's voice. They were all silent for a few seconds, then came Henry's voice.

'He's not dead – look, he's opening his eyes.'

Geoffrey heard, but he was not pleased. Half of him

wanted Maurice to be dead. 'If Maurice is not dead and only hurt, what will he say about me?' he thought. 'And what will mother say? I can never look anybody in the face again.' He felt lonely, and afraid.

Down below on the ground the German girl was crying and laughing at the same time. 'No, he's not dead, no, he's not dead, no–o.'

'He can't speak. He needs some water,' said Henry.

'Yes, somebody must run and get some,' said the father. 'Bill, you go. The vicar's house is nearest.'

Bill ran up to the vicar's house beside the top field,

The German girl was crying and laughing at the same time.

10

where the German governess worked. Soon he came back, followed by the vicar. Maurice drank a little water, and began to make noises, trying to speak.

'What happened to him?' asked the vicar.

Everybody spoke at once, but the German girl's voice was the loudest.

'It was the brother – the other brother,' she cried. 'He knocked him over. I saw him, I was watching.'

'I don't think so,' said the father to the vicar. Then he got down next to Maurice, who was still making little noises. 'Where does it hurt, boy, eh?' he asked, worried.

'Wait a bit,' said Henry. 'Wait until he can speak.'

'Has he broken anything?' asked the vicar.

'He was lucky,' said the farm worker, Bill, 'lucky to fall on this bit of hay, and not the hard ground.'

Maurice could speak a little now, and the father asked him, 'What were you doing, boy? Were you playing around with our Geoffrey? Yes, and where is he?'

On top of the stack Geoffrey stood like a stone.

'I'll have a look on the stack,' said Henry.

Geoffrey did not want his big brother to come up on the stack, so he climbed down, and at the bottom of the ladder stood like a criminal, looking at the ground.

'What were you doing?' asked Henry's cold voice.

'I don't know. Nothing,' Geoffrey said.

'But I saw him!' cried the governess. She was sitting on

the ground, holding Maurice in her arms. 'He knocked him over the side – bouf! like that!'

Henry looked from one brother to the other.

'No, girl,' whispered Maurice, smiling up at her. 'He wasn't near me. I just fell – fell over the side.'

'Oh!' cried the girl, not understanding.

'You just made a mistake,' said the father. 'That's all.'

'Oh no,' she cried. 'I *saw* him.'

Her name was Paula Jablonowsky, and her family came from Poland. She was twenty years old, quick and light as a wild-cat, with a strange, wild way of laughing. She had bright blue eyes and short golden hair. Everybody could see that the vicar hated her.

Maurice's face was still white, but he lay, smiling happily in the girl's arms. She smiled down at him, with her quick, bright smile. Her English was not very good, but there are stronger things than words.

'You say what you like,' she laughed, 'about your brother, about anything.'

'Perhaps you need to go back to the children now,' the vicar said to her, frowning a little.

'I will go soon,' the girl said. She smiled at Maurice again. 'You want to get up now?' she asked softly.

'I'm not in a hurry,' Maurice said, smiling happily.

'She's leaving us soon,' the vicar whispered to the father. 'My wife really doesn't like her.'

12

Maurice lay, smiling happily in the girl's arms.

'Why, is she—?'

'Like a wild thing – she won't do what we tell her.'

Maurice decided to get up, and the girl helped him, with her strong arms. 'You are well,' she cried happily.

'Yes, I'm all right,' he said. 'The fall knocked the breath out of me, that's all.' After a moment he walked a few steps. 'See, father,' he laughed. 'I'm fine now.'

'Fine, fine!' the girl said, her eyes shining.

Maurice laughed, and touched her face gently.

'Don't worry. She's going at the end of three weeks,' the vicar said quietly in the farmer's ear.

13

3

The tramp and the woman

'We're not going to finish that last bit of hay today,' Henry said crossly.

The father still looked worried about Maurice. 'Are you sure you're all right?' he asked.

'Yes, I'm all right. I've told you.'

'Then sit down and rest for a bit. In a while you can get the dinner out for us.'

The men went back to work, and the governess ran back to the vicar's house, to her job with the children. Maurice sat down under a tree. 'I'll marry her,' he thought. 'Yes, I will. I've got fifty pounds, and mother will help me.' For a long time he sat there, thinking about married life. Then he got up and went to get the dinner from the big wagon by the road.

The two fields belonged to the Wookey family, but they were four miles from the home farm. So the father had to bring dinner and tea to the fields every day, and the workers ate there. Cutting the hay usually took about two weeks, and somebody had to sleep in the field at night, to watch the tools. Either Maurice or Geoffrey usually did this.

Mrs Wookey always sent a good dinner, and today was no different. There were two big meat pies, cold potatoes, bread, and a great piece of cheese. Maurice put the food out in the shade of a big tree. Everybody sat down in a circle, and ate their meal.

Everybody sat down in a circle, and ate their meal.

It was good to be out of the burning sun, under the shade of the tree. The men ate and drank silently, the father reading a newspaper, the others eating busily.

Then, 'She's here again!' said Bill. Everybody looked up. Paula was coming across the field, carrying a plate.

'She's bringing something for you, Maurice,' said Henry, laughing at him. Maurice was halfway through a great piece of meat pie and some cold potatoes.

The father laughed too. 'Put that away, Maurice. She'll want you to eat what she's brought for you.'

'Give it here,' said Bill. 'I'll eat it for you.'

Then Paula arrived. 'I bring him some chicken – him!'

The father laughed. 'Put that away, Maurice.'

She gave Maurice a bright smile. Maurice's face turned deep red, and everybody laughed aloud.

The father felt sorry for his shy son. 'Come and sit here by me,' he said to Paula.

'Thank you,' said Paula happily. She sat down next to the father and smiled at him.

'My name,' she said, 'is Paula Jablonowsky.'

'Paula, what?' said the father. The other men laughed. 'Paula, eh? Strange kind of name. My son's name is—'

'Maurice – I know.' She said the name sweetly, and Maurice's face turned an even deeper red.

'Tell me about yourself,' the father said to the girl.

'I come from Hanover, in Germany,' she said. 'My father is a shop-keeper, and I ran away from home because I didn't like him. I went to Paris and I worked in a girls' school there.'

'Did you like it?'

'Oh no – it was so boring! Nothing to do.'

'And do you like life in England?' said the father.

'No – ah, no. The vicar and his wife . . . no, no, no.'

'And what will you do?' the father asked.

'I will go to London, or to Paris. Or get married!' She laughed into the father's eyes.

The father laughed too. 'Get married, eh? Who to?'

'I don't know. I am going away.'

'Do you think you'd like making butter and cheese?'

'Oh yes!' She smiled her quick bright smile, and her eyes shone.

'I think she'd like anything different from her life now,' said Henry. He heard a noise and looked round. 'Hallo, who's this?' he said.

A tramp was crossing the field towards them. He was small, thin, and dirty, with mean little eyes.

'Have you got a bit of work for me?' he called out.

'A bit of work?' said the father. 'Can't you see that we've nearly finished these fields?'

'And you don't know anything about hay-making,' said Henry, coldly.

'I'm a hard worker,' said the tramp. His small eyes looked from father to son, and back again.

'Well, we've got no work for you,' said the father. 'But you can have a bit of something to eat, if you like.'

'Yes, I would,' said the man.

They gave him the last piece of meat pie. He ate it quickly, hungrily. 'That was good,' he said. He did not go away, so they gave him a piece of bread and cheese. Then he asked for a drink of water. He sat down to drink it, but the other men did not talk to him. They did not like him, and had nothing to say to him.

While he sat there, a young woman came into the field and walked down beside the hedge. She was small and finely made. Her clothes were neat and tidy, and her hair was pulled back under a sailor hat. She had a pretty face, but there was a hard, cold look in her eyes.

'Have you got some work?' she asked her man.

'No, they haven't got any work for me. They just gave me a drink of water.'

'Have you got some work?' the young woman asked.

19

He was a mean, hateful little man.

'And do I have to wait for you in the road all day?'

'You don't have to if you don't want to. You can go on. But if you wait a bit, perhaps you'll get something.'

The woman looked for the first time at the men, staring at them, unsmiling.

'Have you had your dinner?' asked the father. 'He's had a lot to eat. You can have some, if you want it.'

'What have you had?' she asked the man angrily.

'A great piece of meat pie, and a great piece of bread and cheese,' said Geoffrey.

The young woman looked at Geoffrey, and he at her. There was a kind of understanding between them. Both of them felt alone in the world. Geoffrey smiled a little, but she was too angry to smile.

'There's some cold potatoes,' Maurice said to the woman. 'You can have some of them.'

She frowned and did not answer. Again she looked at Geoffrey, and again there was a silent understanding between them. Then she turned and walked away.

'We must get back to work,' said Henry. He stood up and stared coldly at the tramp. 'Time to go.'

The tramp stood up too. 'Aren't you going to give me something for her? She's had nothing to eat all day.'

They gave him some bread and cheese. He pushed it into his pocket, and walked away.

4

At night in the hayfield

Geoffrey worked hard all afternoon, cutting the hay, while Maurice worked on the wagon. The brothers did not speak, but the feeling between them was warm and friendly. Geoffrey understood that their little fight would stay a secret – Maurice would not tell.

The sun got hotter and hotter. There was not a breath of wind, and everybody began to feel tired.

'There's another day's work here,' said the father at tea-time, while they sat under the tree.

'Somebody will have to stay the night here then,' said Geoffrey. 'I'll do it.'

'No, I'll do it,' said Maurice.

'You did it last night,' said the father. 'You must get some rest tonight.'

'No, I'm staying,' said Maurice.

'He wants to meet his girl again,' explained Henry.

The father thought about this. 'I don't know . . .'

But in the end Maurice stayed. At eight o'clock, after sundown, the men got on their bicycles, the father got the wagon ready, and everybody left.

Slowly, the evening sky turned dark. The young man stood alone in the field, listening to the sounds of the night. It was still hot, and from the hedges came the rich, sweet smell of wild flowers. Then the moon came out, catching the flowers in its light, and they shone like white ghostly faces against the dark of the hedge.

Higher on the hill, the farm horses, free for the night, were moving around the field. Maurice had an hour to wait before Paula came, and he decided to take a bath in the little river at the bottom of the fields.

He washed himself in the cold water, and it felt good on his warm body. Above him the tall trees by the river whispered in a little wind. 'How beautiful the night is!' he thought. Laughing, he took a handful of white flowers from the hedge, and threw them over himself.

At nine o'clock he was waiting under the tree by the haystacks. He felt both excited, and afraid. She was late. At a quarter past nine she came, running across the field, as light and as quick as a bird.

'Oh, their little girl would *not* go to sleep tonight,' she cried. 'I sat in that bedroom for an hour.' She looked up at the sky and took a deep breath. 'Ah, the night smells so good!' She smiled.

She was full of life, quick and strong at the same time.

'I want' – she could not find the English words – 'I would like – to run – now!'

Maurice ran after her, but he could not catch her easily.

Maurice laughed. 'Let's run, then,' he said.

And in a second she was gone. Maurice ran after her, but he could not catch her easily. At last he caught her by the arm, and they stood together, laughing.

'I can run faster,' she cried happily. 'Yes?'

'No,' he replied, with his deep little laugh. 'No, you can't.' They walked on across the field, and then suddenly saw the three farm horses in front of them.

'We ride a horse?' she said.

'Now?' said Maurice. 'In the dark?'

'Yes, yes,' she cried, 'in the dark!'

Maurice caught one of the horses, put the girl on the

23

horse's back, then climbed up in front of her. She put her arms round his waist.

The horse walked uphill and at the top they stopped and looked round. Clouds were moving across the sky, hiding the moon and the stars. The night lay across the fields and hills like a great dark carpet, with here and there the little lights of a house or a farm.

Maurice could feel the girl's warm arms around his waist. 'Do you want to go back now?' he asked.

'I stay with you,' she answered softly.

Maurice gave a little laugh. He wanted to kiss her, but he was afraid to. The horse moved under them.

Maurice could feel the girl's warm arms around his waist.

'Let the horse go fast,' said Paula. 'Fast!'

'All right then,' Maurice said. He hit the horse's neck. 'Come on, boy, let's go!' he cried.

And away they went down the hill, faster and faster. It was a wild, dangerous, exciting ride. Maurice held on to the horse with hands and knees; Paula held on to Maurice, her arms around his waist, and her face against his strong, warm back.

At last the horse came to a stop. Paula half fell off its back, and Maurice quickly jumped down beside her. They were both laughing, and excited by their wild ride. And suddenly, he had her in his arms, and was kissing her. They did not move for some time. Then, silently, arm in arm, they walked to the haystacks.

The sky was now dark and heavy with cloud. Maurice looked up, and felt a drop of rain on his face.

'It's going to rain,' he said. 'I'll have to put the cover on the new stack.'

He left Paula, and went to the shed in the corner of the field. He pulled out the big heavy cover and pulled it across the ground to the stack.

'What are you going to do?' asked Paula.

'Put it over the top of the stack, to keep the rain out.'

'Ah!' she cried. 'Up there!'

Rain began to fall. It was very dark between the two great buildings of hay. Maurice put the long ladder up the side of the stack, and Paula stared up at the black wall of hay above her.

'You carry the cover up there?' she asked.

'Yes,' said Maurice.

'I must help you,' she said.

And she did. Maurice went first up the ladder, carrying one end of the cover, and Paula climbed up behind him, carrying the other end.

While they were climbing up the ladder, a light stopped on the road by the top field. It was Geoffrey on his bicycle, coming to help his brother with the cover for the haystack. Silently, he pushed his bicycle across the field to the shed. He was afraid to call out. If his brother was with the German girl, he did not want to surprise them together in the dark.

There was no one in the shed. He walked across to the stacks and was nearly there when he heard a noise. The ladder was slowly falling down the side of the stack. It hit the ground with a bang.

'What was that?' he heard Maurice's voice, from the top of the stack.

'Something fell,' came the voice of the German girl.

Maurice lay down and looked over the side of the stack. 'It was the ladder!' he said. 'We knocked it down, when we were pulling the cover up.'

'We're in prison up here?' the girl said, excited.

'Yes. But if I shout, they'll hear at the vicar's house.'

'Oh no,' she said quickly.

'I don't want to,' he replied, with a short laugh.

He began to pull the cover across the top of the stack. Down below, Geoffrey moved quietly round the corner

The ladder was slowly falling down the side of the stack.

of the second haystack. He did not want them to see him. He heard Maurice's voice again.

'One good thing, we won't get wet. We can sit under the cover.'

'Maurice!' said the girl. She sounded worried.

'What is it?' he said gently. 'You'll be all right. Look, the cover's on now. We can sit under this corner.'

'Will I be all right, Maurice?'

'Of course you will. But do you want to go back to the vicar's house? Shall I shout for somebody?'

'No. No, I don't want to go back.'

'Are you sure?' he asked.

'Yes, yes, I am sure.' She laughed.

Geoffrey turned away at the last words, and walked back to the shed. The rain was now falling heavily. He felt miserable, and lonely.

In the shed he took the lamp off his bicycle and shone it round the walls. All the tools lay in one corner, and there was a big wooden box, and a deep bed of hay.

He put the lamp out and threw himself down on the hay. 'I'll put the ladder up for them later,' he thought. He lay there, thinking about his brother's luck, and the German girl, with her strange ways and her quick, bright laugh. 'Why does she like Maurice? Why doesn't she like me? No woman will ever love me,' he thought miserably. 'I'm too slow, I don't have the words.'

5

A meeting in the dark

While Geoffrey lay there, thinking about his life, he suddenly heard a sound that was not the rain. Something was in the shed, moving towards him. For a second, terror filled him, then he jumped up, and caught the thing with his great hands.

It did not fight, just gave a small, unhappy cry.

'Let me go,' said a woman's voice.

'What do you want?' he asked, angrily.

'I thought he was here.' She began to weep, quietly.

'Who? Who did you think was here?' he said.

'My husband. He was here at dinner-time. You saw him.' She tried to pull away from his hands. 'Let me go.'

'It's you!' said Geoffrey, in surprise. 'Are you looking for that dirty little tramp that was here at dinner?' He still held her with both hands, but more gently now. 'Where did he leave you?'

'I left him – here,' she said. 'I've seen nothing of him since.'

Geoffrey gave a short laugh. 'That's a good thing, isn't it? Why would you want to see him again?'

29

'He's my husband – and he's not going to run away if I can stop him.'

Geoffrey was silent, not knowing what to say.

'Your clothes are wet,' he said at last.

'That's not surprising, is it, in this rain? But he's not here, so I'll go.'

'You're cold, aren't you?' said Geoffrey. 'I can feel it. You're shaking with cold.'

She did not answer. He did not know what to say.

'Wait a minute.' He found his bicycle lamp, lit it, and shone the light on her. He saw a white, tired face. Her old sailor hat and her brown coat were black with rain. Drops of water fell from her wet skirt onto her shoes.

Geoffrey shone the light on her.

30

He looked worried. 'You're wet right through,' he said. 'Why don't you stay in here until the rain stops?'

No answer.

'You can take your wet things off, and put a blanket round you. There's a horse-blanket in the box here.'

He waited, but there was still no answer.

He put the lamp down, opened the wooden box, and took out a big grey blanket. 'Come on,' he said, kindly. 'Take your hat and coat off, and put this round you.'

Slowly, she took off her hat and coat and put the blanket round her. She was shaking all over with cold.

'Is something the matter with you?' he said, worried.

'I've walked to Bulwell and back,' she said tiredly, 'looking for him. I've eaten nothing since this morning.' She did not weep – she was too tired, too miserable.

'You've had nothing to eat?' he said. He went back to the box. There was food in there – bread and cheese. He cut some bread and put a big piece of cheese on it.

She sat down on the end of the bed of hay, and slowly began to eat. Then he gave her a drink of water, and saw that she was still shaking.

'Can't you get warm?' he asked.

'I will in a minute. Don't you worry. I'll go soon. I'm taking your seat – are you staying here all night?'

'Yes. But you must stay, and get warm. I've got to go and see that the haystacks are all right. Take your wet things off, and get warm with that blanket round you.'

'I'll go in ten minutes. This is your place, and I'm not going to push you out. It's not right.'

'You're not pushing me out,' he said. 'I'll come back when I've looked at the stacks.'

He went. A minute later, she put the lamp out. He stood between the stacks, listening. There was only the soft rain and the dark night all around him. Everything was still, silent, black – like death, he thought.

He found his way back to the shed and went in. 'Are you all right?' he said. He lit the lamp again. Her small face looked up at him, out of the grey blanket.

'You don't need a lamp,' she said. 'Lie down and get your night's rest. I can sit at this end, out of your way.'

He put the lamp out, and sat down on the hay, at the other end. Then he asked, 'Is he really your husband?'

'He is!' she answered, in a hard little voice.

'Do you follow him because you like him?' He was afraid to ask, but he wanted to know.

'I don't – I wish he was dead.' Her voice was coldly angry. Then, 'But he's my husband.'

He gave a short laugh. 'Not much of one,' he said. 'Have you been married long?'

'Four years. Since I was eighteen.'

'And do you just move about, all the time?' he asked.

'He says he's looking for a job. But he doesn't like work.

32

'I can sit at this end, out of your way,' she said.

He was a wagon-driver when I married him. He left that
job when the baby was only two months old, and I've not
had a kind word or a day's rest since then.'

'And where's the baby?'

'It died when it was ten months old.'

After that they were silent. At last Geoffrey said slowly, 'You've had a hard life.' He looked at her, but saw nothing in the dark. 'What will you do now?'

'I'll find him. He's not going to get away.'

'But why don't you leave him?'

'Because he's *not going to win.*'

He listened to her hard voice, and felt miserable for her. He could not see her; they were just two voices in the black night.

'Are you warm now?' he asked, half afraid.

'A bit warmer – but my feet are still terribly cold.'

'I can warm them with my hands. Shall I?'

'No, thank you,' she said, coldly. Then she felt sorry. He was kind, he was trying to help. 'But they do hurt.'

'Put them in my hands, then.'

His large, strong hands closed round her icy feet and held them. She felt his warm breath on her toes.

'Do they feel any better yet?' he asked, after a while.

She did not answer. She put out her hand and touched his hair. His hand came up to find hers, but found her face, which was wet with tears. Gently, his fingers followed the tears down her cheeks.

'What's the matter?' he said, in his slow, deep voice.

She put out both her arms and pulled his head to her. Four lonely, miserable years were suddenly behind her; she was no longer old before her time. Suddenly, it was possible to hope again, to be young, to be happy. She wept long and silently, holding Geoffrey's head close to her, with her wild tears falling on his hair.

Geoffrey sat still, full of wonder, full of love. When at last she stopped weeping, he put his arms around her, gently. And in a while, they kissed, his first love kiss.

She wept long and silently, holding Geoffrey's head close to her, with her wild tears falling on his hair.

35

6

Breakfast in the hayfield

When Geoffrey woke, a cold morning light was coming into the shed. Outside, a heavy mist lay across the field, hiding the trees and the hedges.

The woman was sleeping in his arms, and he held her gently, staring out into the mist, still full of wonder and love. He would never be afraid or lonely again, with her beside him.

Then he looked down at her, and saw that she was open-eyed, watching him. She had golden-brown eyes, that immediately smiled into his. He also smiled, and softly kissed her.

After a time, he asked shyly, 'What's your name?'

'Lydia,' she said.

'Lydia,' he said slowly, liking the sound of it. 'My name's Geoffrey. Geoffrey Wookey.'

She smiled at him, and for a while they were silent.

'We couldn't get married, could we?' he asked.

'No.'

He thought deeply about this for some time.

'Would you go to Canada with me?'

'Perhaps you'll think differently in two months' time,' she replied quietly.

'I'll think the same. I won't change,' he said, hurt.

She watched him. She would not push him, would not hurry him. She would stay with him, but he must decide, he must do what he wanted.

'Haven't you got any family?' he asked.

'A married sister at Crick. I can go there, if you want me to. I'll get a job on a farm perhaps.'

'And then, in the spring, we'll go to Canada. You will come with me, won't you?' he said, hopefully.

'When the time comes.'

She did not trust him yet, and he understood why.

'I'll give you some money before you go to Crick,' he said. 'You'll go past our farm on your way.'

'I don't need it. I've got some money.'

Her answer worried him. Perhaps she didn't need him or his help. He began to feel afraid. 'Can I write to you? What name shall I use?'

'Mrs Bredon.'

'Your married name!' he said, with a short, hard laugh. 'I'll never see you again, will I?'

She put her arms round him and held him. There were tears in her eyes, but he was still worried, unsure.

Outside the mist was getting thinner. He remembered Maurice then, and told her about him.

'Oh,' she said. 'You must go and put the ladder up for them, you must!'

'All right. But wait here, and see Maurice. Then I can tell him about us.'

She agreed to wait, and he went out to the haystack. There was no sound from above, and he could see nothing. He put the ladder back up in the same place, and then went along the hedge, looking for firewood.

Then he heard Maurice's voice. 'Well, look at that!'

'Well, look at that!' said Maurice.

'Look at what?' That was the girl. 'The ladder – oh! You said it fell down!'

'It did,' said Maurice. 'Well, I heard a bang, and I couldn't see the ladder, or feel it.'

'You said it fell down – and it wasn't true!'

'It *was* true—' he began.

'Not true, not true!' she cried. 'You are bad, a mean person – mean, mean, mean!' She was wildly angry.

'All right then!' Maurice was also angry now. 'Are you coming down?'

'No! I will not come with you. You are mean – you tell me untrue things. I don't want you!'

Geoffrey, looking through the hedge, saw Maurice on the ladder. He climbed down, then stood at the bottom. 'Come on, I'll hold the ladder for you,' he called.

'No!' she cried, like a wild cat.

He waited for a while, but she did not come. 'Then stay there till you're ready,' he said quietly, and walked away. On the other side of the stack he met Geoffrey.

'What are you doing here?' he said.

'I've been here all night,' Geoffrey replied. 'I came to help you with the cover, but the cover was on, the ladder was down, and I couldn't find you.'

'Did you put the ladder up?'

'Yes, I did it just now.'

Maurice stood still, thinking. Geoffrey tried to find the

words to tell him about Lydia. He began, stopped, began again, and at last told the story of his night.

'Oh!' said Maurice. He began to smile.

'The man is nothing, just a tramp, but she's different,' said Geoffrey. He wanted Maurice to understand.

'You please yourself, what you do,' said Maurice. He was quiet, worried, not like himself.

'What's the matter?' asked the older brother. It was strange to see Maurice like this, and for once Maurice was not laughing at him.

'Nothing,' said Maurice.

They went together to the shed. The woman was putting the blanket away in the box. She was washed, and tidy, and looked very neat and pretty.

'Hello,' said Maurice. He smiled, shyly. 'It was good you found somewhere to get out of the rain last night.'

'Yes,' she replied.

'Can you get more firewood?' Geoffrey asked him. It was a new thing for Geoffrey to ask Maurice to do something. Maurice agreed, and went out into the field. He did not go near the stack, afraid of meeting Paula.

At the shed Geoffrey was making a fire, while Lydia got out coffee and bread from the box. Breakfast was nearly ready when Paula arrived. She had no hat on, there were bits of hay in her hair, and she was white-faced. She did not look her best.

'Ah – you!' she cried, seeing Geoffrey.

'Hello!' he answered. 'You're out early.'

'Where's Maurice?'

'I don't know, he'll be back soon.'

Paula was silent. 'When did you come?' she asked.

'Last night, but I didn't see anybody. I got up just now, and put the ladder up, ready to take the cover off.'

Paula understood, and was silent. When Maurice returned with some wood, she was warming her hands

When Maurice returned, Paula was warming her hands at the fire.

41

at the fire. She looked up at him, but he would not look at her. Geoffrey met Lydia's eyes, and smiled. Maurice held out his hands to the fire.

'You are cold?' asked Paula, softly.

'A bit,' he answered, friendly but not too friendly.

The four of them sat round the fire, drinking their smoky coffee, eating their bread and cheese. All the time Paula watched Maurice's face hopefully, and he watched the fire. He was gentle, but he would not look at her. And Geoffrey smiled and smiled at Lydia, who watched him with her golden-brown eyes, and did not look away.

The German girl got back into the vicar's house that morning, and her night out in the hayfield stayed a secret. A week later, she was engaged to Maurice, and when her last three weeks with the vicar's family were finished, she came to live at the Wookey farm.

Geoffrey and Lydia stayed true, one to the other.

GLOSSARY

bang *(n)* a sudden very loud noise

blanket a cover that you sleep under, to keep you warm

breath taking in or sending out air through your nose and mouth

cheek one of the two round parts of your face under your eyes

cheese yellow or white food made from milk

cover *(n)* a thing that goes over another thing, to keep it dry, etc.

engaged if two people are engaged, they have agreed to marry

feelings something that you feel inside yourself (e.g. angry, sad)

fool a person who is stupid or who does something stupid

fork a large tool with points at one end, used for farm work

frown *(v)* to move your eyebrows together to make lines on
  your forehead (you frown when you are worried or angry)

gentle quiet and kind

ghostly like a ghost; not real

governess a woman employed to teach the children of a rich
  family in their home

hate *(n)* a strong feeling of not liking someone; opposite of 'love'

hay grass which is cut and dried, and used as food for animals

hay-maker somebody who cuts and dries grass to make hay

haystack (stack) a very big pile of hay, built in a tall 'box' shape

hedge a line of small trees that makes a kind of wall round a field

icy like ice; very, very cold

kiss *(v)* to touch someone with your lips to show love

ladder two tall pieces of wood, with shorter pieces between
  them, used for climbing up something

lamp a thing that gives light

lean *(v)* to put or rest your body against another thing

light *(adj)* not heavy, easy to lift or move; not dark in colour

mean *(adj)* not kind

miserable   very sad or unhappy

mist   thin cloud near the ground that is difficult to see through

neat   with everything in the right place; tidy

pie   meat (or vegetables, or fruit) inside a pastry case

pretty   nice to look at

shade *(n)*   a place out of the sunlight (under a tree, behind a high wall, etc.)

shed   a small building for keeping tools, animals, etc.

shy   not able to talk easily to people that you do not know

stare *(v)*   to look at someone or something for a long time

tears   water that comes from the eyes when you cry

terror   the feeling when you are very, very afraid

throw (past tense **threw**)   to move your arm quickly to send something through the air

tool   a thing that you hold in your hand and use to do a job (e.g. a fork is a farm tool)

tramp *(n)*   a person with no home or job, who goes from place to place

trust *(v)*   to feel sure that someone is honest and good

vicar   a priest in the Church of England

wagon   a kind of open 'car' pulled by a horse or horses

waist   the part around the middle of your body

wave *(v)*   to move your hand from side to side, to say hello or goodbye

weep   to cry

whisper *(v)*   to speak in a very soft, quiet voice

wonder *(n)*   a feeling that you have when you see something very strange or beautiful or surprising

Before Reading

1 **Read the story introduction on the first page of the book, and the back cover. What do you know now about the story? Tick one box for each sentence.**

	YES	NO
1 The story takes place on a cold winter's day.	☐	☐
2 Maurice and Geoffrey are cutting the hay.	☐	☐
3 The two brothers like the same woman.	☐	☐
4 Geoffrey is pleased about Maurice and Paula.	☐	☐
5 Wind and rain are bad for new hay.	☐	☐
6 Maurice is luckier in love than Geoffrey.	☐	☐
7 Geoffrey finds it easy to talk about his feelings.	☐	☐

2 **What happens to the people in this story? Can you guess? Choose words to complete this passage.**

Maurice meets *Paula / another woman* in the hayfield *that night / the next day*. Geoffrey meets *Paula / another woman* in the hayfield *that night / the next day*. She is very *angry / unhappy*, and when Geoffrey is *kind / unkind* to her, she *laughs / cries*. Geoffrey *kisses / does not kiss* her.

By the next day, *everybody / nobody* is *miserable / in love*, and the story ends *happily / unhappily*.

ACTIVITIES

<hr>

While Reading

Read Chapter 1, then match these people with the sentences. (You can use the names more than once.)

Geoffrey / Maurice / the German girl

1 _____ slept in the hayfield last night.
2 _____ has never kissed a girl.
3 _____ works at the house near the hayfield.
4 _____ is interested in _____, not _____.
5 _____ pushes _____ off the haystack.

Before you read Chapter 2, what do you think happens? Choose one answer for each sentence.

1 Maurice . . .
   a) breaks a leg.   b) is all right.   c) breaks his neck.
2 The German girl . . .
   a) cries.   b) kisses Maurice.   c) hits Geoffrey.
3 Geoffrey . . .
   a) feels pleased.   b) feels angry.   c) feels afraid.

Read Chapters 2 and 3. Are these sentences true (T) or false (F)? Rewrite the false ones with the correct information.

1 Maurice was badly hurt by his fall.

2 Paula said that Geoffrey knocked Maurice over the side of the haystack.

3 Maurice told his father about the fight with Geoffrey.

4 Geoffrey did not say anything about the fight.

5 Paula worked for the vicar, but the vicar did not like her.

6 At dinner Maurice asked Paula lots of questions.

7 A tramp came into the field and asked for food.

8 The father gave the tramp something to eat.

9 The tramp's young woman had something to eat.

10 Geoffrey understood how the young woman felt.

Before you read Chapter 4, can you guess who will stay at the hayfield when the men stop work?

1 Geoffrey   2 Maurice   3 Henry

Read Chapter 4, then put these sentences in the right order for the chapter.

1 Paula helped Maurice carry the cover up the ladder.

2 After the others left, Maurice washed himself in the river.

3 Geoffrey went to the shed and lay down on the hay bed.

4 The ladder fell down and Geoffrey left it there.

5 Paula came, and rode with Maurice across the hayfield.

6 Paula and Maurice stayed on top of the haystack.

7 Geoffrey arrived and walked across to the stacks.

8 It began to rain.

Before you read Chapter 5, *A meeting in the dark,* which of these people do you think meet in this chapter? Choose some names from this list.

Maurice	the father	the vicar's wife
Geoffrey	Paula	the tramp
Henry	the vicar	the tramp's woman

Read Chapter 5. Who said these words? Who or what were they talking about?

1 'He's not going to run away if I can stop him.'
2 'This is your place, and I'm not going to push you out.'
3 'Do you follow him because you like him?'
4 'I can sit at this end, out of your way.'
5 'It died when it was ten months old.'
6 'I can warm them with my hands. Shall I?'

How does the story end? Before you read Chapter 6, can you guess which of these sentences are true? Choose as many as you like.

1 Geoffrey forgets about the ladder and goes home.
2 The four young people have breakfast together.
3 Maurice asks Paula to marry him.
4 Paula goes to London and later Maurice follows her.
5 The tramp's wife goes back to her husband.
6 Geoffrey asks the tramp's wife to go away with him.

After Reading

1 **Here is Farmer Wookey telling his wife about the day. Put their conversation in the correct order and write in the speakers' names. Farmer Wookey speaks first (number 4).**

1 _____ 'No, it was the wife of a tramp who was looking for work. But I felt sorry for the poor girl.'

2 _____ 'That's the girl who's working for the vicar, isn't it? Do you know her name?'

3 _____ 'Strange? Why, what happened?'

4 _____ 'It's been a strange day today.'

5 _____ 'Why? What was the matter with her?'

6 _____ 'Paula – something. I think Maurice likes her.'

7 _____ 'Well, in the morning Maurice and Geoffrey were up on the haystack, and Maurice fell off.'

8 _____ 'Who was the other? Was it Bill's daughter?'

9 _____ 'She looked so unhappy. Her husband was a mean little man. She can't have much of a life.'

10 _____ 'Oh, no! Is he all right? Did he hurt himself?'

11 _____ 'Well, I think he has. She's a bright little thing. But not the only pretty woman in the field today.'

12 _____ 'No, he's all right. That little German girl saw him fall and came running down to see him.'

13 _____ 'Does he now! I'd like him to find a nice girl.'

2 Here is a new illustration for the story. Find the best place in
the story to put the picture, and answer these questions.

The picture goes on page _____.

1 Who is Maurice calling to on top of the haystack?

2 Where has the ladder been all night?

3 Who put the ladder up?

Now write a caption for the illustration.

Caption: _____

3 Use the clues to complete this crossword with words from the story (all the words go across). Then find two hidden words (four letters or more) in the crossword.

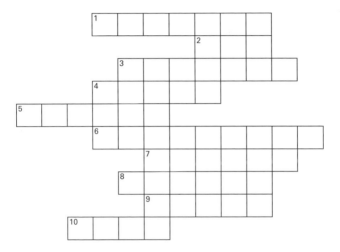

1 You sleep under this on a bed to keep warm.

2 Very, very cold.

3 To speak in a very soft, quiet voice.

4 Water that comes from the eyes when you cry.

5 Nice to look at.

6 Very sad or unhappy.

7 The feeling when you are very, very afraid.

8 You use this to climb to a high place.

9 They put this over the haystack, to keep the rain off.

10 A farm tool which is used to pick hay up.

The hidden words are _____ and _____.

4 Here are the two women in the story talking about their plans. Complete each passage with words from this list. Then say who is speaking, and who they are talking to.

baby, Canada, cheese, engaged, farm, Germany, hate, kind, leave, marry, miserable, sorry, spring, stay, true, trust, wants

1 'We're _____ now, Maurice and I. So I'm not going back to _____ when I _____ here. I'm going to live at the Wookey _____ and learn to make _____. I won't be _____ to leave here. You and your wife _____ me. Isn't that _____?

2 He's a good, _____ man, and I think I can _____ him. I can't _____ him, but I've had a _____ life since the _____ died. So if he still _____ me to, I'll go to _____ with him in the _____. Can I _____ with you until then?

5 What do you think is important when you choose someone to spend your life with? Add two more ideas of your own to this list, then choose the five most important ideas and number them 1 to 5 (with 1 for the most important).

The right person is somebody who . . .

· has a good job   · is kind

· is the same age as you   · is clever

· comes from a good family   · works hard

· laughs at the same things as you · is happy

· thinks about other people   · is loving

ABOUT THE AUTHOR

David Herbert Lawrence was born in 1885 near Nottingham, England, one of five children in a poor family. His father was a coal miner, but his mother was an ex-schoolteacher and wanted her son to study and escape the life of a poor miner. Lawrence went to Nottingham University and trained to be a teacher, but had to stop teaching after a serious illness in 1911.

His first novel, *The White Peacock*, was published in 1911, and in 1912 he fell in love with Frieda von Richthofen Weekley, the wife of his old professor in Nottingham. They ran away to Germany, and married in 1914. They were always travelling, always short of money, and had a passionate and stormy life.

Lawrence died young and was often ill, but he wrote a great number of books – travel books, poems, short stories, and novels, including *Sons and Lovers* (1913), *The Rainbow* (1915), and *Women in Love* (1921). At the time many people were shocked by these novels because of their frank descriptions of sex.

After living in Sri Lanka, Australia, the United States, and Mexico, Lawrence, now seriously ill, returned to Europe with Frieda in 1925. He finally died in the south of France in 1930. His last novel, *Lady Chatterley's Lover*, was published in Italy in 1928 but was banned in England and America because of its descriptions of sex. It was finally published more than thirty years later, after a famous six-day legal trial.

'Love among the Haystacks' was one of Lawrence's earliest short stories, written in about 1913. It was loosely based on a night Lawrence spent camping under a haystack, after a day helping a friend's family with the hay-making.

OXFORD BOOKWORMS LIBRARY

Classics • Crime & Mystery • Factfiles • Fantasy & Horror
Human Interest • Playscripts • Thriller & Adventure
True Stories • World Stories

The OXFORD BOOKWORMS LIBRARY provides enjoyable reading in English, with a wide range of classic and modern fiction, non-fiction, and plays. It includes original and adapted texts in seven carefully graded language stages, which take learners from beginner to advanced level. An overview is given on the next pages.

All Stage 1 titles are available as audio recordings, as well as over eighty other titles from Starter to Stage 6. All Starters and many titles at Stages 1 to 4 are specially recommended for younger learners. Every Bookworm is illustrated, and Starters and Factfiles have full-colour illustrations.

The OXFORD BOOKWORMS LIBRARY also offers extensive support. Each book contains an introduction to the story, notes about the author, a glossary, and activities. Additional resources include tests and worksheets, and answers for these and for the activities in the books. There is advice on running a class library, using audio recordings, and the many ways of using Oxford Bookworms in reading programmes. Resource materials are available on the website <www.oup.com/elt/bookworms>.

The *Oxford Bookworms Collection* is a series for advanced learners. It consists of volumes of short stories by well-known authors, both classic and modern. Texts are not abridged or adapted in any way, but carefully selected to be accessible to the advanced student.

You can find details and a full list of titles in the *Oxford Bookworms Library Catalogue* and *Oxford English Language Teaching Catalogues*, and on the website <www.oup.com/elt/bookworms>.

THE OXFORD BOOKWORMS LIBRARY
GRADING AND SAMPLE EXTRACTS

STARTER • 250 HEADWORDS

present simple – present continuous – imperative –
can/cannot, must – *going to* (future) – simple gerunds ...

Her phone is ringing – but where is it?

Sally gets out of bed and looks in her bag. No phone. She looks under the bed. No phone. Then she looks behind the door. There is her phone. Sally picks up her phone and answers it. *Sally's Phone*

STAGE 1 • 400 HEADWORDS

... past simple – coordination with *and, but, or* –
subordination with *before, after, when, because, so* ...

I knew him in Persia. He was a famous builder and I worked with him there. For a time I was his friend, but not for long. When he came to Paris, I came after him – I wanted to watch him. He was a very clever, very dangerous man. *The Phantom of the Opera*

STAGE 2 • 700 HEADWORDS

... present perfect – *will* (future) – *(don't) have to, must not, could* –
comparison of adjectives – simple *if* clauses – past continuous –
tag questions – *ask/tell* + infinitive ...

While I was writing these words in my diary, I decided what to do. I must try to escape. I shall try to get down the wall outside. The window is high above the ground, but I have to try. I shall take some of the gold with me – if I escape, perhaps it will be helpful later. *Dracula*

STAGE 3 • 1000 HEADWORDS

... should, may – present perfect continuous – *used to* – past perfect –
causative – relative clauses – indirect statements ...

Of course, it was most important that no one should see
Colin, Mary, or Dickon entering the secret garden. So Colin
gave orders to the gardeners that they must all keep away
from that part of the garden in future. *The Secret Garden*

STAGE 4 • 1400 HEADWORDS

... past perfect continuous – passive (simple forms) –
would conditional clauses – indirect questions –
relatives with *where/when* – gerunds after prepositions/phrases ...

I was glad. Now Hyde could not show his face to the world
again. If he did, every honest man in London would be proud
to report him to the police. *Dr Jekyll and Mr Hyde*

STAGE 5 • 1800 HEADWORDS

... future continuous – future perfect –
passive (modals, continuous forms) –
would have conditional clauses – modals + perfect infinitive ...

If he had spoken Estella's name, I would have hit him. I was
so angry with him, and so depressed about my future, that I
could not eat the breakfast. Instead I went straight to the old
house. *Great Expectations*

STAGE 6 • 2500 HEADWORDS

... passive (infinitives, gerunds) – advanced modal meanings –
clauses of concession, condition

When I stepped up to the piano, I was confident. It was as if I
knew that the prodigy side of me really did exist. And when I
started to play, I was so caught up in how lovely I looked that
I didn't worry how I would sound. *The Joy Luck Club*